LNER
SIX-COUPLED TANK
LOCOMOTIVES
1948–68

ERIC SAWFORD

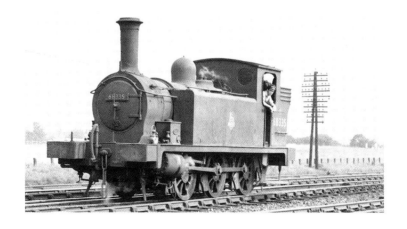

First published in 2006 by
Sutton Publishing Limited . Phoenix Mill
Thrupp . Stroud . Gloucestershire . GL5 2BU

British Library Cataloguing in Publication Data
A catalogue record for this book is available from the British Library.

ISBN 0-7509-4346-7

Front endpaper: N7 no. 69617, pictured at Cambridge. This engine was withdrawn in July 1960.   21.8.57

Back endpaper: L1 no. 67734, fitted with Westinghouse brake and vacuum ejector.   17.6.52

Title page photograph: The short-wheelbase J88s were introduced in 1904 for dock shunting and for use on lines with tight curves. No. 68335, built in 1909, was one of two to receive vacuum ejectors, all the others being steam brake only.   24.8.55

Typeset in 10/12 pt Palatino.
Typesetting and origination by
Sutton Publishing Limited.
Printed and bound in England by
J.H. Haynes & Co. Ltd, Sparkford.

Contents

Introduction

The years immediately following the nationalisation of the railways in 1948 had much to offer the railway enthusiast. Steam was still very much in charge, and although a few diesels were to be seen, they were regarded by many as a novelty. How all this was to change as the 1950s progressed.

For several years during the early 1950s I regularly travelled to and from Kings Cross. There was always plenty to see in those now-distant days. The principal passenger, mixed traffic and goods locomotives were of course very interesting, but as this volume is concerned only with tank engines, I shall concentrate on these. My journeys to London commenced at Huntingdon, and one of the first places of note was Hitchin. The small locomotive depot was situated to the east of the station building, and was not easily seen unless you were standing on the south end of the platform. Space was a problem here, but a few locomotives could usually be seen in the sidings; quite often L1 tanks would stand there, especially if they were undergoing minor repairs. There was sometimes an ex-Great Eastern 0–6–0T, with perhaps an N2 0–6–2T taking on fresh supplies of coal and water.

Just a few miles further on was Hatfield, another small shed. In the mid-1950s its allocation comprised 2 J52 saddle-tanks, 4 N1 0–6–2Ts, 8 N2s and 15 N7s. The depot here was to the west of the main line; again it was small, with space very much at a premium.

Nearer London, there were numerous sidings to keep an eye on and I well remember J52s and N1s pottering about in various small goods yards. In the carriage sidings I saw mostly N2s. The last shed my train passed before arriving at Finsbury Park was Hornsey. This was a sizeable depot, and its allocation was made up entirely of tank locomotives, supplemented by a small number of J6 0–6–0s. In the very early 1950s a considerable number of veteran J52s were still active here; when these and the N1s were withdrawn, they were replaced by J50s. Towards the end of the decade these were joined by five J94 0–6–0STs of Ministry of Supply origin. Throughout the 1950s a considerable number of N2s were to be found at Hornsey. Freight locomotives working to Ferme Park also used Hornsey for refuelling before their return working.

The principal shed of the district was Kings Cross. Unfortunately it could not be seen, although engines moving to and fro were often visible. Later a locomotive yard was added at Kings Cross, principally to service locomotives arriving on passenger services and to save them having to go to Kings Cross depot.

In the London area the N2s seemed to be everywhere. They mostly worked suburban services, and their characteristic sharp exhaust note echoed distinctively under the large, cavernous roof of Kings Cross station. On many occasions I have travelled on a main line train with an N2 running alongside on a suburban service. These trains were frequently heavily loaded and the N2s had to cope with rising gradients, tunnels and fairly frequent stops. They also required a fair turn of speed to comply with the tight start-stop timings.

There was a constant requirement for empty stock workings, and the N2s proved ideal for the task, although I also saw N1s and even the odd J50 on this work from time to time. In due course diesel locomotives took over both the suburban duties and the stock workings, and for me Kings Cross was never the same afterwards.

During the early 1950s Liverpool Street was an ideal location to see N7s at work, heading Enfield, Chingford and other suburban services. Also at this station J69 0–6–0Ts could be seen on pilot duties.

Busy times at Nottingham Victoria as A5s nos 69806 and 69825 stand ready for departure. Both these locomotives were allocated to Colwick depot, and members of the class were used on Grantham and Derby trains.   6.7.51

In the 1950s only two classes of 0–6–0STs were to be found on the Eastern Region. These were the veteran J52s and the J94s purchased by the LNER from the Ministry of Supply. J52 no. 68835 is seen here at Doncaster, while a J94 can just be seen behind it.   23.9.56

With several Royal Air Force stations in the immediate area during the 1950s, a 'leave' train was operated from Huntingdon East station on a Friday evening using a close-coupled suburban set. Here no. 67745 heads this service. At this time only the Midland line platform was regularly used by passenger services, but these ended in June 1959. 6.8.54

Wherever you travelled on British Railways at this time you would soon come across six-coupled tank locomotives, not only hauling local passenger, branch and cross-country services, but also working in the many shunting yards and sidings that existed in those days.

In 1911 J.G. Robinson introduced his 4–6–2 tank design, which later became the LNER class A5s. These were principally intended to replace smaller engines on the Marylebone suburban services, which were having difficulty in handling the increased loads. Twenty-five were built at Gorton Works between 1911 and 1917, and they soon proved themselves to be sturdy 'good pullers' and well liked by enginemen. These were followed in 1923 by a further batch of ten, also from Gorton.

Shortly after Grouping in 1923 the need arose for additional passenger tank engines for the north-east. This resulted in a further thirteen A5s being ordered, this time from a private company, Hawthorn, Leslie. They were delivered in 1925/6. These particular engines had smaller boiler mountings and a few detail differences. Their duties included the difficult and steeply graded coast route to Scarborough. By nationalisation in 1948 A5s were to be found at a number of sheds, as by this time the Marylebone services had largely been passed over to Thompson L1 2–6–4Ts. The decision to do so was not particularly welcome among some of Neasden depot's enginemen.

Three classes of 4–6–2T built by the North Eastern Railway passed into British Railways ownership.

Another of the Doncaster-built N7/3s was no. 69727, seen here fresh from general overhaul at Stratford Works and resplendent in its lined-out livery. It would not have remained in this condition for long. Built in 1928, it was to complete thirty-two years' service before being cut up at Stratford.　　　　　7.5.55

In 1907 the A6 class was introduced by William Worsdell. Ten were built, all at Gateshead Works. They were principally intended to work on the difficult North East Coast line. The first A6 was withdrawn in June 1947 and by 1951 eight others had gone, leaving just no. 69796. The station pilot at Hull, this engine remained active until 1953 when it was also condemned.

Considerable numbers of coal trains were worked from the many collieries in the north-east of England to docks along the coast, where the coal was transferred to shipping for onward transportation. To avoid tender-first working, twenty large 4–6–2Ts, later to become the LNER class A7, were introduced. All were built at Darlington, and the first appeared in 1910. All passed into BR ownership. In their final years these engines were allocated to two Hull depots. Withdrawals commenced in 1951, with the last members of the class going for scrap in 1957.

In 1913 a class of forty-five 4–4–4Ts was introduced on the North Eastern Railway, principally for short-distance passenger services. They were never very successful, often encountering problems in difficult weather conditions, especially with heavy loads on rising gradients. In 1931 Gresley decided to rebuild these engines as 4–6–2Ts, known as class A8. It was a wise decision. The rebuilds were powerful and reliable on suburban trains and well able to cope with the demanding coastal route. In the early 1950s A8s could be found at a number of sheds in the north-east. As in other areas, though, dieselisation soon resulted in these locomotives being placed in store. Withdrawals commenced in late 1957, the last members of the class going in 1960.

In 1930 Gresley introduced the V1 class 2–6–2Ts, all built at Doncaster Works. The last ten were built in 1939/40 as class V3, with higher boiler pressure, and in due course the majority of the V1s were rebuilt as V3s. In the early 1950s all the V1s and V3s were allocated to the north-east and Scotland. Those that had previously been in the southern area moved north, and were generally replaced by L1s. Withdrawals of V1s and V3s did not commence until 1960. By then work for them was becoming scarce, as it was for so many other locomotives. By the end of 1964 the V class tanks had all been condemned.

In 1945 the LNER announced a five-year locomotive modernisation plan, including the introduction of 110 L1 class 2–6–4Ts (although in the event only 100 were built). They were to be constructed at Darlington Works, with a few being supplied by the North British Locomotive Company and R. Stephensons & Hawthorns. The first engine, no. 9000, later to become no. 67701, appeared in May 1945 in fully lined-out apple green livery. Extensive trials on all types of train were carried out with this engine in England and Scotland. Orders had already been placed for further locomotives, but none was actually delivered until BR had taken over. In due course L1s were allocated to many Eastern and North Eastern Region depots. They were successful engines capable of a fair turn of speed. The first withdrawal came in late 1960, and just two years later the entire class had been withdrawn. The headlong rush to diesel power resulted in a comparatively short working life for a class of engines that no doubt would have given excellent service for many years.

Technically this is not a good photograph but it is of considerable interest as it shows L3 2–6–4T no. 69064 passing Huntingdon with the Little Barford power station empties. This engine was transferred to New England in the late 1940s to work these trains. However, it was not a success on this work, mainly because of braking problems on the 1 in 200 descent to Huntingdon. If the signals were against it, and especially if the rails were wet and greasy, the L3 had great difficulty in stopping the train. No. 69064 did not remain long on these duties before being returned to Neasden, and I cannot recall ever seeing another picture of this locomotive working this train. 14.11.50

The J71 was designed by T.W. Worsdell and introduced in 1886. The entire class of 120 locomotives was built at Darlington Works between 1886 and 1895. This is no. 68235 at Darlington. Some members of this class were noted for their long service, and this engine itself clocked up seventy-three years.   7.7.56

There had originally been another L1 class, which was redesignated the L3 class to make way for the Thompson engines. The original L1 was a Great Central design, and twenty examples were built between 1914 and 1917. Officially classified 5F, many were withdrawn shortly after nationalisation. One member of the class with which I was to become very familiar was no. 69064. In 1947 this engine was transferred to New England to work the heavy coal trains to Little Barford power station. Most of the route was easy going, with the exception of the long falling gradient of 1 in 200 from Abbots Ripton to Huntingdon. If the signals were against it at the latter, the engine was hard pressed to stop its train in time. As it was not popular with enginemen, the L3 remained on this duty for only a comparatively short period before returning to Neasden. Unfortunately I managed to take only one photograph of this engine. The Little Barford trains were subsequently taken over by WD 2–8–0s, although an 04 2–8–0 occasionally appeared.

A huge number of six-coupled tank locomotives were used only for shunting, and these had the J prefix. The Great Eastern J67 class had spread far and wide, with examples to be found as far north as Scotland. There was of course a large concentration of these engines in the London area, especially at Stratford. The principal shunting locomotives of the north-east were the J71s and J72s; here again examples of the latter were also to be found in Scotland. The J77 class 0–6–0Ts were rebuilds of Fletcher 0–4–4Ts. There was also a more powerful class of 0–6–0Ts, the J73s.

North of the border my attention was particularly drawn to the short-wheelbase, outside cylinder 0–6–0Ts of class J88. These had tall, distinctive chimneys and 3ft 9in driving wheels.

In the early 1950s A5 no. 69820 was one of those members of the class allocated to Immingham depot. It is seen here at Lincoln station, and to judge from the headcode it carries it is in charge of an express passenger service. The first coach of its train was a veteran clerestory vehicle. 26.8.51

Ready to commence its journey to Hitchin, L1 no. 67744 stands in Huntingdon goods yard. When given the right of way it had to cross both the Up and Down main lines to join the Up slow. The early evening was always a busy time for express traffic. 16.9.54

It was several years before 'LNER' disappeared from all the Eastern Region locomotives, especially the tank engines used on pilot duties and shunting work. J68 no. 8645 is seen here at Cambridge.   30.5.51

Withdrawn locomotives from the London area usually travelled to Doncaster under their own steam. Some travelled at quiet periods during the night but on Sunday mornings at around 10 or 11 a.m. it wasn't uncommon to see one stop to take water. J50 no. 68991, seen here at Huntingdon, was the last of the class to be built, being completed at Gorton Works in August 1939.   8.61

Complete chaos ensued on the East Coast main line when L1 no. 67740 became derailed on a crossover near Huntingdon no. 2 signal-box. The New England crane was in attendance when this picture was taken, and was ready to commence lifting.   19.5.51

Several were allocated to St Margaret's depot, Edinburgh. Most of their work was done from the sub-sheds for which this depot was responsible. At South Leith, for example, the J88s worked on the docks alongside veteran class Y9 0–4–0STs, which ran with permanently attached wooden tenders. You could always find these engines at what was known as the 'small tank roundhouse' at St Margaret's, which at that time was open with a turntable.

The Board of Trade insisted that locomotives used on public roads must be fitted with cowcatchers and have their motion and valve gear shielded by steel-plate side aprons. One line where this applied was the Wisbech & Upwell Tramway. Initially services here were worked by Y6 class 0–4–0 'Tram' engines that had been built at Stratford Works over a four-year period from 1883. Increasing traffic eventually led to the need for more powerful engines. In October 1903 the first of the 0–6–0 J70 'Tram' engines, designed by J. Holden, was completed at Stratford Works. Engines of both these classes had a wooden superstructure, in many ways resembling a guard's van. They had two cylinders with Walschaerts valve gear, slide valves and a boiler pressure of 180psi. The first examples built were supplied to Ipswich and Yarmouth for dock work, with three going to Wisbech. Later this number was increased to five. With both Y6s and J70s available, the Y6s were principally used on passenger trains while the more powerful J70s were allocated to the goods trains, which in the height of the fruit season were heavily loaded.

On 31 December 1927 passenger services on the Wisbech and Upwell Tramway were withdrawn. This meant that just two engines were required to handle the remaining traffic, except during the busy fruit season. Five J70s still remained in service when the Drewry diesel-mechanical 0–6–0s were introduced in 1952. The last scheduled steam turn ran on 4 July 1952. Subsequently four J70s and the sole remaining Y6 were sent to March, where they were lined up at the back of the shed. I was fortunate enough to photograph them here in November 1952, although they were not in the best of positions. As a safeguard no. 68222 was kept at Wisbech to cover any diesel failures; this was just as well, as it was called upon on a number of occasions. But it too left in March 1953 and was to end its working life at Ipswich, from where it was withdrawn in January 1955.

Of the five locomotives at March, the Y6 was never to work again, being condemned in November 1952. J70s nos 68220 and 68217 did not survive for long, being withdrawn in February and March 1953 respectively. Nos 68222, 68223 and 68225 were transferred to new locations, but all were withdrawn in 1955, ending their days where they started at Stratford Works.

In the early 1950s I made several visits to Cambridge depot and on each occasion J66 no. 68383 was present. In all, fifty members of the class were built, only one going into service stock. Cambridge had a long association with the class, with as many as seven being allocated there at times. By 1948 only eighteen members of the class were still in service, with a further three in departmental service at Stratford Works. In 1950 just two remained: no. 68372, which was to be withdrawn in February 1951, and no. 68383. No. 68383 was transferred to Staveley for a short period before its withdrawal in October 1955, when it was the last in revenue service. On withdrawal it was sent all the way back to Stratford, where it stood for some time in the yard before being cut up.

The 1950s were the swan-song of steam on British Railways. During the decade many lines were closed, and this, together with the headlong rush into dieselisation, soon resulted in rows of redundant steam locomotives. Some depots still covered the chimneys with pieces of tarpaulin sheet and greased the motion, and it was by no means unusual to find stored locomotives with their tanks full and coaled up. Very few were to work again. Tank locomotives were withdrawn in large numbers during the late 1950s and early 1960s. Long gone are the periods of almost continuous shunting work in the larger yards, which was once such a ubiquitous feature of our railways.

Chapter One
Passenger Tanks

During the period immediately before nationalisation discussions took place to establish a uniform classification covering locomotives of all regions. In due course it was decided, in principal, to follow the existing LMS system. This used a power classification ranging from 0 to 8, together with a letter indicating the type of work. After various modifications the new classification basically consisted of passenger, mixed traffic and freight locomotives, with a further listing of 'unclass' covering the Sentinels.

There were only a small number of six-coupled passenger tanks, comprising the Great Central's A5s and the North Eastern Railway's A6s and A8s, the latter being rebuilds of a 4–4–4T design introduced in 1913. Many, such as the L1 2–6–4Ts, were more often seen on passenger services and were in fact classified as mixed traffic. The P-passenger classification also included a number of tank locomotive classes with four-coupled driving wheels, but these are outside the scope of this book.

In the 1950s increasing numbers of diesel railcars and locomotives resulted in many steam locomotives becoming redundant. By the end of the decade their numbers had been dramatically reduced, with many of the older classes soon becoming extinct.

The A5 4–6–2Ts were in charge of services in many parts of eastern England. No. 69822, seen here outside Grantham shed, was a Colwick engine and would return on a Nottingham–Derby service. These graceful locomotives were well liked by enginemen and capable of a fair turn of speed. 7.8.54

(*Opposite, top*): The Great Central A5 4–6–2Ts were introduced in 1911, principally to replace the smaller tank locomotives working the Marylebone suburban services at the time. Between 1911 and 1917 twenty-one were constructed, among them no. 69811, seen here at Hull Botanic Gardens shed. Between 1923 and 1927 the LNER built another twenty-three, all with reduced boiler mountings. 22.5.55

(*Opposite, bottom*): In the mid-1950s Boston had an allocation of four A5 4–6–2Ts, among them no. 69808. At this time these attractive engines were used in many parts of Lincolnshire on local passenger services. Built at Gorton in 1911, this locomotive did not receive a side-window cab until 1926. It was withdrawn in November 1960. 13.3.55

In May 1957 A5 no. 69828 was transferred to Colwick. I photographed it at Doncaster, so perhaps it had been sent for attention in the works. No. 69828 was one of a batch of ten built at Gorton in 1923; it remained in service until November 1958, by which time it had moved again, this time to Langwith Junction.   25.8.57

(*Opposite, top*): A8 no. 69856 in steam in the repair part of West Auckland shed. Note the pulley wheels on the back wall driving machine tools, and the large circular smoke hoods. This A8 was rebuilt from a 4–4–4T in September 1934 and remained in service until December 1959.   7.7.56

(*Opposite, bottom*): This picture illustrates the massive proportions of the A8 4–6–2Ts, which were used on local passenger services. This is no. 69867, photographed at Hull Botanic Gardens shed. Built at Darlington in 1914 as a 4–4–4T, it was rebuilt in July 1936 and remained in service until December 1959.   22.5.55

One A8 4–6–2T, no. 69877, was allocated to Malton depot in the mid-1950s. It is seen here at the head of an engineer's train. The Malton A8 was often used to assist heavy passenger trains heading for the coast. No. 69877 was withdrawn from Scarborough in December 1959.   22.5.55

(*Opposite, top*): This run-down class A8, no. 69861, was photographed awaiting entry to Darlington Works. It received a general overhaul and was to survive until withdrawal in June 1960. No. 69861 was allocated to Malton depot, one of two to be found there.   8.7.56

(*Opposite, bottom*): Busy times at Sunderland. A8 no. 69853 was one of several engines that had just arrived on shed and were awaiting servicing. Six A8s were allocated to the depot at this time and their duties included through trains to Bishop Auckland. Numbers of the class built up at Sunderland as they were displaced elsewhere. No. 69853 was withdrawn in January 1960.   8.7.56

Sunshine and shadow in Scarborough shed, where A8 4–6–2T no. 69867 was under repair. Built in March 1914 as a 4–4–4T, this engine was rebuilt as a 4–6–2T in July 1936. It was one of five allocated to Scarborough in the mid-1950s, where their duties included the demanding coast line. The rapid changeover to diesel railcars brought about the demise of many A8s. No. 69867 was withdrawn in December 1959.   23.9.56

Whenever I visited depots in the north-east I seemed to find A8s under repair. This is no. 69862 at Middlesbrough, with a 'not to be moved' sign on the front of the footplate. Like its classmates, it was built originally as a 4–4–4T in 1914, being rebuilt in January 1933 as an A8 4–6–2T. It remained in service until July 1958.   8.7.56

Chapter Two
Mixed Traffic Designs

The 0–6–2T wheel arrangement was very common during the 1950s. In the London area N2s and N7s were responsible for many suburban services at Kings Cross and Liverpool Street. The earlier N1s, at one time familiar in the area, were already in the process of being transferred elsewhere or had been condemned.

The Great Central N5s were still to be seen on passenger trains in some parts of the country but the majority of the class were used on empty stock workings or shunting duties. N5s were to be found at many sheds, some of them in the London Midland Region.

North of the border former North British N15s were to be found at a number of depots, especially those in the Edinburgh and Glasgow areas. The North Eastern Railway was represented here by the N8 and N9 classes, although these had already been considerably reduced in number.

In 1930 Sir Nigel Gresley introduced the V1 class 2–6–2Ts. These were followed in 1939 by the V3s, which were similar in design but had a higher boiler pressure. In LNER days these locomotives had worked in what was to become the Eastern Region. By the 1950s they were only to be found in the north-east and north of the border in Scotland, where they were widely used on suburban and local passenger workings.

In 1945 Edward Thompson introduced the L1 class 2–6–4Ts. In BR days these were classified 4MT, the same as the numerous tanks of this wheel arrangement found on the London Midland Region. The L1s were included in the 1945 five-year modernisation plans, with a total of 110 scheduled; in fact only 100 were completed. The pioneer L1, no. 9000 (later 67701), was the sole example until 1948, when production commenced at Darlington, with some also being produced by the North British Locomotive Company. The last examples were built by R. Stephenson & Hawthorns in 1949/50, well into BR days. The first example was subjected to a very comprehensive series of trials on former GN, GE and GC lines and proved to be powerful and economical on coal consumption. However, it was not satisfactory on heavy goods trains owing to braking problems, especially on a falling gradient.

The L1s were introduced late in the day, and all too soon dieselisation was to result in a shortage of work for them. The first member of the class to be withdrawn completed just over twelve years' service, being condemned in 1960. Within two years all had gone.

The N5 class was introduced principally for trip and shunting work. Following Grouping in 1923, some engines of this type were regularly used on local passenger work. T. Parker introduced them in 1891 as a development of the earlier N4 design. No. 69296, pictured at Sheffield Darnell, was built at Gorton in 1896 and remained in service until December 1960.   24.6.56

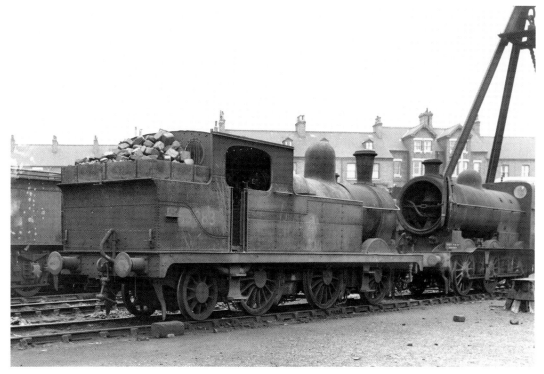

Retford depot consisted of two buildings, one of Great Central and the other of Great Northern origin. These were considered to be a single depot with the shedcode 36E. The Great Northern shed was rebuilt, and was the last to close in June 1965. Here N5 no. 69283 waits under the shear legs with a J6 0–6–0.   25.8.57

Trafford Park was a London Midland Region depot. In the mid-1950s its allocation consisted of thirty-seven engines, mostly Great Central designs. They included a number of N5 0–6–2Ts, including no. 69255. Built by Beyer Peacock & Company in 1893, it remained in service for sixty-three years. 16.10.55

Three ex-Great Central Railway veterans at Trafford Park. N5 0–6–2T no. 69347 stands between another N5 and J10 0–6–0 no. 65181. The N5s were the standard shunting locomotives of the Great Central and were also used on local goods duties. No. 69347 was among those built at Gorton Works, being completed in December 1900. 16.10.55

The 'flowerpot' chimney fitted to the N5 0–6–2Ts can be clearly seen in this picture of no. 69275 at Lincoln. This was one of the class built by Beyer Peacock & Company in 1894. Time had almost run out for this engine, as it was withdrawn three months after this picture was taken.   14.8.55

Private contractors were frequently used to construct new locomotives for the pre-Grouping railway companies. A considerable number of N5s were built by Beyer Peacock & Company, including no. 69305, completed in 1893. Seen here at Mexborough, this engine moved to Walton for its final years and was withdrawn in January 1960.   24.6.56

N4/2 no. 69231, built by Neilson & Company in 1890, awaits the scrapman's cutting torch at Doncaster. Presumably the painted crosses over the number and emblem had been added at its home shed when it was condemned. Withdrawn in October 1954 from Sheffield Darnall, it was among the last in service. In total fifty-five N4 class 0–6–2Ts were built by the Manchester, Sheffield & Lincolnshire Railway between 1889 and 1892; in 1897 they all became part of the Great Central. Only twenty-two were taken into British Railway stock in 1948, with the last of them being withdrawn in 1954. The N5 class was a development of these engines. 7.11.54

In total sixty-two N8 class 0–6–2Ts were built, thirty-six of which survived to nationalisation. This number was rapidly reduced so that only a few were left in service in the mid-1950s. No. 69390, seen here at Tyne Dock, was built in 1889 and was the last survivor of the class, being withdrawn just three months after this picture was taken. Some of the N8s were used on passenger duties.   8.7.56

(*Opposite, top*): Resplendent after a general overhaul, N15 no. 69152 is seen here at the 'old tank' roundhouse at St Margaret's. This locomotive was built by the North British Locomotive Company in 1912 and had steam brake only. Most N15s were employed on goods work, but some served as incline pilots for banking passenger trains out of Glasgow Queen Street. On the track adjacent to the N15 the locomotive has buffers made of blocks, as did many of the small tank engines found here.   21.8.55

(*Opposite, bottom*): The N15 class locomotives were built over a long period, the last in LNER days by R. Stephenson & Company and at Cowlairs Works. No. 69192, seen here at Dunfermline, was completed in 1920 by the North British Locomotive Company; it was originally built with a vacuum ejector but this was removed in the early 1920s.   22.8.55

N1 no. 69467 at Hornsey. Such engines had been a familiar sight for many years but they were already nearing their end; in August 1956 the last N1 left Hornsey. No. 69467 was withdrawn in July 1956.   3.1.54

(*Opposite, top*): N1 0–6–2Ts were once a familiar sight in the London area but by the early 1950s they were becoming scarce, and in 1954 several moved north to various depots. No. 69435 was photographed at Hornsey. This engine retained its condensing gear throughout its working life. Built at Doncaster in 1907, it was among the first batch constructed. Withdrawal came in March 1955.   3.1.54

(*Opposite, bottom*): N1 no. 69443 awaiting its next duty at Bradford shed. Built in 1910, this engine was originally fitted with condensing gear, but this was removed in November 1929. The N1s were principally used on local passenger workings in the West Riding. The surviving members of the class were all withdrawn in 1959, among them no. 69443.   13.5.56

Originally N1 no. 69481 was fitted with condensing gear. This was later removed, although the inverted 'U' bend in the side tank was still in position, presumably blanked off. By 1956 only three of the surviving N1s were still in the London area, the other eighteen all having been transferred to Yorkshire.   13.5.56

(*Opposite, top*): The N1 0–6–2Ts had a long association with passenger workings in the West Riding. Time had almost run out for no. 69481, seen here at Ardsley shed, as it was withdrawn in the same month that this picture was taken. Originally this engine was fitted with condensing gear, but this was later removed on a works visit.   13.5.56

(*Opposite, bottom*): Twelve V class 2–6–2Ts were allocated to Heaton depot in the mid-1950s, with others at Gateshead and Blaydon, all within the same motive power district. These engines were principally used on local passenger services. No. 67635 was still a V1 class, and was not converted to V3 until October 1960. In September 1963 it was withdrawn, ending its days at Darlington Works.   8.7.56

Two months before this picture was taken no. 67646 had been converted to a V3 class. It is seen here awaiting servicing at Heaton shed. Designed by Gresley, these 2–6–2T tanks were widely used on suburban services in the north-east.   8.6.56

(*Opposite, top*): V1 class no. 67618, in pristine condition after a general overhaul at Darlington Works, waits to return north of the border to its home shed, 65E Kipps. This engine was converted to a V3 in September 1958. Withdrawn in December 1962 after months in storage at Polmont, it was returned to Darlington Works in November 1963 and cut up.   8.7.56

(*Opposite, bottom*): V1 class no. 67647 was built at Doncaster in 1935, and the hopper-type bunker can be clearly seen in this picture taken at Heaton. This engine was rebuilt to V3 class in December 1959 and remained in service until January 1963. After a short period in storage at Darlington Works, it was cut up in June 1963.   8.7.56

Eastfield shed had an allocation of 139 locomotives of many classes and so was a fascinating place to visit in the early 1950s. V1 class 2–6–2Ts were often to be seen coming and going. No. 67602 was a Doncaster-built engine that was completed in October 1930. It was never converted to a V3 and was withdrawn in May 1962.   26.8.55

(*Opposite, top*): Wherever possible, I tried to photograph ex-works locomotives. This is V3 no. 67687 fresh from a general overhaul in Darlington Works and ready to return to its home depot after 'running in' trials. This engine was one of ten built new as V3s, and it must have returned for another general overhaul as it was not withdrawn until December 1962.   7.7.56

(*Opposite, bottom*): Gresley V1 class 2–6–2Ts were used to work suburban trains in the Glasgow area and seventeen engines were allocated to Eastfield, including no. 67671. The majority of the class were rebuilt as V3s; this engine was among the exceptions. It was withdrawn in July 1960.   26.8.55

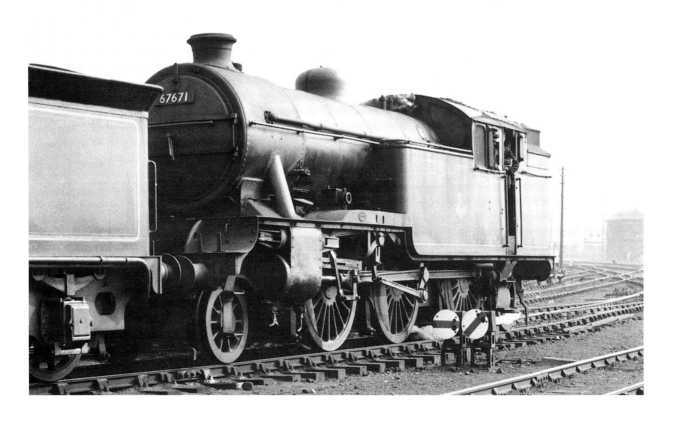

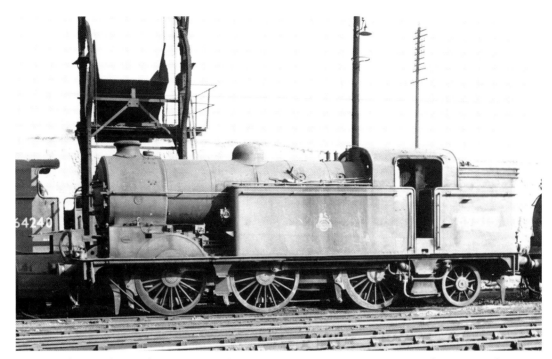

Built by the North British Locomotive Company in 1921, N2 no. 69515, seen here at Hitchin, was originally fitted with condensing gear, but this was removed in August 1928. Only ten members of the class were built at Doncaster Works in 1920/1. The majority were constructed by private companies, including the North British, Hawthorn Leslie and the Yorkshire Engine Company. No. 69515 was withdrawn in July 1959.   14.10.56

Fresh from general overhaul at Doncaster, N2 no. 69513 would soon be ready to return to its home depot, Hornsey. Engines travelling to and from works moved mostly at night or early on a Sunday morning. No. 69513 had been repainted in a fully lined-out livery.   23.9.56

A heavy pall of smoke was hanging over Kings Cross shed when I took this picture of N2 no. 69490, in lined-out livery. This engine was built at Doncaster in 1920 and fitted with condensing gear from new. It remained in service until July 1959, ending its days at Doncaster the following month.   3.1.54

Most of the Kings Cross N2s were overhauled at Doncaster Works but no. 69490 had just received its general overhaul at Stratford, and now, less than two years later than the previous picture, was painted in an unlined black livery.   13.11.55

I had become very familiar with the N2 class 0–6–2Ts and I certainly did not expect to find one at Aberdeen Ferryhill. No. 69503 had been allocated to Kipps shed before moving to Aberdeen. In fact, several N2s were to be found at Scottish depots. This engine was withdrawn in January 1957 and cut up at Kilmarnock Works two months later.   24.8.55

(*Opposite, top*): N2 no. 69560 stands ready to take out the stock of an express that had just arrived at Kings Cross, thus releasing the locomotive for servicing. Still lettered British Railways, the N2 was in unlined livery. This engine was built by Beyer Peacock & Company in 1925 and was never fitted with condensing gear.   9.7.53

(*Opposite, bottom*): A once familiar sight at principal stations was the 'wheel tapper' walking the length of a train before its departure or on its arrival, tapping each wheel with a long-handled hammer to check for cracks. In this picture he has reached the end of the train and is deep in discussion with the driver of N2 no. 69560.   9.7.53

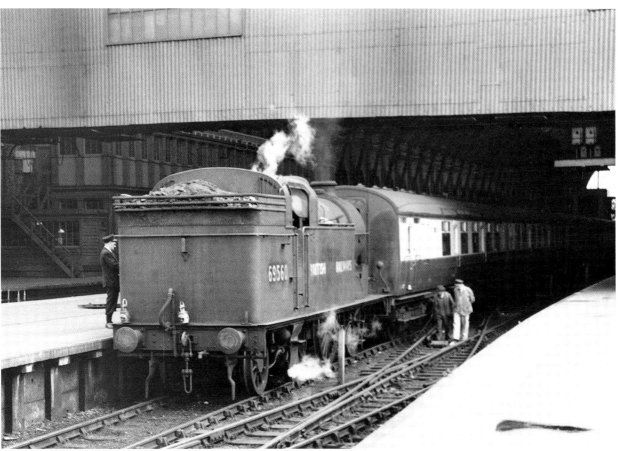

N2 no. 69559, photographed at Stratford shed, was constructed by Beyer, Peacock & Co in 1925. It was not built with condensing gear. This N2 was withdrawn from service in July 1957.   7.5.55

Surrounded by parts of scrapped locomotives, N2 no. 69519 awaits its fate on the Doncaster Works scrap road. This was formerly a Kings Cross engine. Work had already started on dismantling the engine; quite what had happened to the front footplating is not known.   10.11.57

The N2s with their sharp exhaust note were a very familiar sight at Kings Cross working suburban services and also empty stock. No. 69575 is seen here heading a Hertford train. 13.5.51

One unusual working at St Ives in the early 1950s was a service that commenced there and ran on Saturday lunchtime only. It was worked by an N7 0–6–2T. Here no. 69713 of Bishops Stortford depot stands ready for departure. 11.11.50

The final batch of N7s, including no. 69722, was built at Doncaster in 1927/8. They had round-topped fireboxes, Westinghouse brakes and vacuum ejectors from new, and were classified N7/3. Seen here at Stratford, fresh from general overhaul and in lined-out livery, this engine was to remain in service until December 1960.   7.5.55

(*Opposite, top*): N7 no. 69609 was originally built with a Belpaire firebox. It was completed at Stratford Works in October 1921, but in August 1948 it was rebuilt with a round-topped firebox and reclassified N7/4. This picture was taken at Stratford. No. 69609 remained in service until April 1958.   7.5.55

(*Opposite, bottom*): Signs of hard work can be seen on the bottom of the smokebox door of N7/4 no. 69614, pictured here at Stratford Works. It was built in 1923 with Westinghouse brake and vacuum ejector, and its condensing gear was removed in 1936. A further change took place four years later when it was rebuilt with a round-topped firebox. This engine remained in service until December 1960.   7.5.55

For several years two preserved locomotives were stored at Neville Hill shed, Leeds. N7 no. 69621 was the last of the class to be built at Stratford, being completed in March 1924. The remainder of the N7s were built at Gorton and Doncaster Works and by two private companies. In the background is K4 no. 61994 *The Great Marquess*.   20.3.66

(*Opposite, top*): Stratford had over 400 locomotives in its allocation and was frequently very smoky, especially on dull, windless days. N7 no. 69623 had just arrived back on shed after a general overhaul. This was almost certainly the last overhaul this engine received as it was withdrawn in February 1959.   13.11.55

(*Opposite, bottom*): In the mid-1950s I made several visits to Stratford, on each occasion finding ex-works N7s present. This is no. 69625 in rather gloomy conditions. This engine was one of the large number allocated there.   13.11.55

For a number of years N7 no. 69617 was a Stratford engine but in February 1957 it was transferred to Cambridge, where this picture was taken. In March 1958 it was on its travels again, this time to King's Lynn. Nine months later it went to Colchester, a year later returning to Stratford from where it was withdrawn in July 1960.   21.8.57

(*Opposite, top*): Standing out among the other grimy locomotives at Stratford shed, N7 no. 69637 had received a general overhaul and was ready to return to its home shed, Hatfield. This engine was built at Gorton and completed in April 1926. This was probably its last overhaul as it was condemned in March 1959. Still a Hatfield engine, it went back to Stratford Works, never to return.   7.5.55

(*Opposite, bottom*): In the 1950s it was by no means unusual to find locomotives that were in the process of receiving running repairs dumped in the shed yard until they could be restored to service. This was the case with N7 no. 69680 at Stratford, where the bearings from the middle set of driving wheels had been removed. No. 69680 was a Colchester engine and remained in service until December 1960.   13.11.55

In the 1950s two types of 0–6–2T were responsible for many suburban services out of the two main Eastern Region London terminal stations. The N7s, of which no. 69702 is a typical example, were to be found at Liverpool Street and Kings Cross. The N2s were easily recognised by their condensing equipment, visible in this picture taken at Stratford.   7.5.55

(*Opposite, top*): The massive coaling plant at Stratford shed looms over N7/5 no. 69647. With an allocation of over 400 engines, Stratford was the largest shed in the British Isles and covered a huge area. It closed in September 1962, with its last few serviceable locomotives being transferred to March depot.   7.5.55

(*Opposite, bottom*): In this picture of no. 69611 at Stratford the Westinghouse brake can be clearly seen on the side of the smokebox. This engine originally had condensing gear, but this was removed in December 1936. Rebuilding to N7/4 took place in April 1940, and withdrawal came in November 1960.   7.5.55

N7 no. 69601 was the second of the class to be built, being completed at Stratford in February 1915. In LNER days it was classified N7/GE. Originally built with a Belpaire firebox, it was rebuilt with a round-topped boiler in November 1944 and reclassified N7/4. Unlike most of the early N7s, this engine was built with a superheater. It was in the process of being repaired at Stratford when this picture was taken, and the smokebox door was tied up with string.   7.5.55

(*Opposite, top*): Two N7s were built in 1915 but it was to be six years before construction started again. No. 69603 was among those completed at Stratford in 1921. Further N7s were produced until 1928 at three LNER works, Stratford, Gorton and Doncaster, while two private builders – R. Stephenson & Company and W. Beardmore & Company – also made some examples. The class eventually numbered 124 locomotives. No. 69603 was built with Westinghouse brake. Note also the tall chimney fitted to the early engines. This engine was withdrawn in July 1959.   7.5.55

(*Opposite, bottom*): In the early 1950s 105 N7s were allocated to Stratford shed, including N7/3 no. 69732. This was the penultimate locomotive of the class, being constructed at Doncaster in 1928. By the mid-1950s most were in work-stained condition, as seen here, unless they had recently had an overhaul.   7.5.55

No. 69647 was one of the Gorton-built engines. Initially classified N7/1, it became an N7/5 when it was rebuilt in November 1943 with a round-topped firebox. Constructed with Westinghouse brake and vacuum ejector, this engine remained at Stratford until it was withdrawn in November 1960. It was cut up at the nearby works two months later.   7.5.55

(*Opposite, top*): L1 no. 67746 awaiting attention in the yard at Hitchin. Several members of the class were allocated to this depot, where their duties included outer suburban services and local pick-up goods. This class totalled 100 locomotives, the first appearing in 1945. Withdrawals were rapid in the 1960s, and the last disappeared in 1962.   14.10.56

(*Opposite, bottom*): L1 no. 67722 at Cambridge, gleaming like a new pin. Built at Darlington Works, this engine was completed in June 1948. It was finished in LNER green livery, and in fact was the last of the class to be painted green. Judging by its condition and its smart, black, lined-out livery, it was probably repainted not long before this picture was taken.   30.5.51

The Huntingdon pilot arrived back from St Ives with a goods train in the early afternoons, and any wagons destined for onward movement were sorted out, with any going south being included in the Hitchin goods which departed at around 5pm. Here L1 no. 67741 awaits departure time. In the background is a loading gauge, once a familiar sight in goods yards.   1.4.55

Fresh from a general overhaul, this is L1 no. 67744 at Huntingdon. These engines were fitted with self-cleaning smokeboxes and electric lighting. This 100-strong class first appeared in 1945, but it was not until after nationalisation that construction restarted, the last example being delivered in 1950.   23.4.55

L1 2–6–4T no. 67741 pulls out of Huntingdon goods yard with the early evening pick-up freight for Hitchin. Although this turn was booked for an L1, on occasions J6 0–6–0s and even for a short period Fowler 2–6–4Ts were also used.   5.5.55

Stratford L1 2–6–4Ts were a familiar sight at Cambridge, working stopping passenger services. Here no. 67729 has rejoined its train of close-coupled stock and stands ready to pull into the platform for its return journey to London Liverpool Street.   14.11.51

In 1945 the LNER produced its five-year modernisation plan, which included the introduction of the new L1 class. No. 67734, seen here at Huntingdon, was fitted with Westinghouse brake and vacuum ejector. Most of the engines seen working on the East Coast main line at this time were steam brake engines with vacuum ejector. This locomotive was transferred to Stratford shortly after this picture was taken.   17.6.52

(*Opposite*): L1 no. 67719 of Lowestoft depot stands over the ashpit at Cambridge depot. It had just received a general overhaul and was in the process of working back to its home depot. The electric lighting, generator and Westinghouse pump can be seen in this picture.   14.4.52

Huntingdon East station had three platforms; out of the picture on the right was the one used by the Kettering–Cambridge service. The two platforms pictured here did not have any regular services after 1953, when the local Huntingdon–St Ives service was withdrawn. As can be seen, the platforms were on a sharp curve with check rails. L1 no. 67745 stands with the RAF leave train, which ran on Fridays only at that time.   6.8.54

(*Opposite, top*): Hitchin shed was very limited for space. The main building was located behind the Up platform, with sidings extending to the southern end. It was not a large depot, with an allocation of just thirty engines during the mid-1950s, eight of which were L1 2–6–4Ts, including no. 67791, seen here with J67/2 no. 68529.   3.1.54

(*Opposite, bottom*): During the early 1950s a number of the Kings Cross–Peterborough services were worked by Hitchin L1s but as more B1s became available, these eventually took over the duties. Here L1 no. 67745 approaches Huntingdon with an early evening train.   26.4.54

Hitchin depot had eight L1 2–6–4Ts in its allocation in the mid-1950s. One regular turn was a pick-up goods to and from Huntingdon. Here no. 67741 stands in the goods yard ready to commence its return journey.   10.8.54

The wagons for the early evening pick-up goods were already sorted by the Huntingdon pilot and made up into a train. This usually resulted in the crew of the L1 having time on their hands. The driver of L1 no. 67741 was intent on watching me take photographs.   10.8.54

The L1 class locomotives were fitted with electric lighting and self-cleaning smokeboxes – note the SC plate below the shedplate. No. 67730 was among those fitted with Westinghouse brake and vacuum ejector. The Westinghouse pump can be seen in front of the side tank. Locomotives from no. 67740 onwards had steam brake and vacuum ejector. The working life of the L1s was cut short by the introduction of diesel multiple units. 13.7.56

Stratford L1 no. 67730 runs slowly through Cambridge station, carrying a white disc instead of a lamp, as was usual on the Great Eastern section. Eleven L1s were allocated to Stratford. No. 67730 was built at Darlington in 1948 and had a fairly short working life of just fourteen years.   13.7.54

(*Opposite, top*): Most L1s ran bunker-first when working outer suburban services to save time turning the locomotive. This is a mid-afternoon train leaving Huntingdon behind no. 67746. The small building on the left was a timekeeper's office.   16.7.54

(*Opposite, bottom*): L1 no. 67741 proceeds slowly through Huntingdon station to take on water at the platform end. This L1 was built by the North British Locomotive Company in 1948 and was fitted with steam brake and vacuum ejector. It remained in service until December 1962.   6.7.54

Having taken on water at Huntingdon, L1 no. 67744 has to join its train. The L1s used on the East Coast main line had steam brake and vacuum ejector. The North British Locomotive Company built this engine in 1948; it was in service for just fourteen years.   16.9.54

(*Opposite, top*): Running light engine, L1 no. 67745 arrives at Huntingdon ready to work a goods train to Hitchin. The trackwork in this picture is interesting as it shows the connection from the goods yard to the Up slow line. The goods yard has long since gone, the site now being occupied by a car park.   31.8.54

(*Opposite, bottom*): The L1 class 2–6–4Ts were classified 4MT, although they were more commonly seen on passenger workings. No. 67744, a Hitchin engine, is seen here at Huntingdon. In the background is the large water tank with chimney that for years was a well-known feature here.   16.9.54

For some considerable time in the mid-1950s a pick-up goods was worked from Hitchin to Huntingdon. Here L1 2–6–4T no. 67790 awaits departure from Huntingdon goods yard. It had to cross over the main lines to reach the Up slow line. The usual locomotives on this turn were L1 2–6–4Ts and J6 0–6–0s. For a short time LMR Fowler 2–6–4Ts that were on loan to Hitchin were also used.   14.6.56

Chapter 3
Freight and Shunting Locomotives

The largest tank locomotives that were taken into British Railways ownership were eight-coupled designs principally used on hump shunting and short trip workings. There were two exceptions. The A7 4–6–2Ts were introduced in 1910 by the North Eastern Railway principally for short-haul working from collieries to port loading facilities. Twenty were built at Darlington in 1910/11. Withdrawals were heavy in the first years of the 1950s, with the last going in 1957. The Great Central Railway also had a large tank design, LNER classification L1 (later L3). Twenty were built, with just one failing to make it into BR ownership. By 1954 there were just three survivors, all of which were withdrawn in the same year.

There were several classes of 0–6–0T, with the J50 and ex-Ministry of Supply J94 0–6–0STs classified 4F. The Great Eastern J68s and Great Northern J52 saddle tanks were listed within the 3F rating. The majority of 0–6–0T designs still active in the 1950s were in the 2F classification, exceptions being the J71s, J88 dock tanks, ex-Great Eastern J70 'tram' engines, and other odd locomotives in the 0F category.

The mid-1950s saw the start of a period of rapid change. The number of diesel shunters was increasing rapidly, replacing many shunting locomotives. Massive inroads were soon made into the remaining steam locomotives and by the 1960s the picture was very different.

J50 no. 68980, seen here at its home shed, Doncaster, was one of the batch built at Gorton in 1938/9. These were classified J50/4, and had a larger bunker with a coal capacity of 5tons 3cwt (later reduced to 4tons 10cwt). The J50/4 engines were fitted with vacuum brakes. This engine was withdrawn from service in February 1960.   23.9.56

J50 no. 68926 completed its service at Hornsey, one of several members of the class transferred there to replace withdrawn J52s. It is seen here at Doncaster in rather battered condition; the front end of the tank had certainly been knocked about. Built in 1922, no. 68926 completed forty years' service before withdrawal in 1962.   13.11.55

Most of the J50s in the London area were allocated to Hornsey depot. When this closed in July 1961, some of the surviving examples moved to Kings Cross or other sheds. No. 68991 is seen here leaving Huntingdon on its final journey having been withdrawn from service.   8.61

Throughout the 1950s and early 1960s a steady stream of tank locomotives from the London area made their final journey north to Doncaster Works for scrapping. Among them was J50 no. 68991. It is seen here taking water at Huntingdon on a Sunday morning. It would almost certainly have gone on shed at New England to take on coal and water, and to clean the fire.   8.61

J50 no. 68911 at Copley Hill depot. Built in 1919 as a J51/2 class, it was rebuilt as a J50/2 in August 1930. Withdrawn in November 1960, it was transferred to departmental stock in February 1961 as no. 10. This is where it ended its days, along with six others. All the departmental J50s were withdrawn in May 1965.   13.5.56

(*Opposite, top*): Hornsey shed provided shunting locomotives for the numerous yards to be found in the area during the 1950s. Its allocation at this time included twenty-seven J50 0–6–0Ts, these engines having increased steadily as veteran J52 saddle tanks were withdrawn. No. 68983 was among the last batch built; completed at Gorton in 1939, it was withdrawn in April 1962.   3.1.54

(*Opposite, bottom*): General clutter and an iron-wheeled barrow surround J71 no. 68239, engaged on shunting work at Darlington. Built there in 1887, this was another member of the class to achieve a very long working life, in this case sixty-nine years. Not all of the class survived to be taken into BR stock, a considerable number being withdrawn in the 1930s.   7.7.56

The shunting tanks of classes J71 and J72 allocated to West Auckland were all steam brake engines. No. 68685 had 18 x 24in cylinders (larger than the 17 x 24in cylinders of its classmates), which gave it a higher tractive effort of 18,790lbs.   7.7.56

Wherever you went in the North-Eastern Region you would invariably come across examples of J71 and J72 shunting tanks. With the collieries and heavy industry to be found there at the time there was plenty of work for these engines, at least until the steadily increasing numbers of diesel shunters took over. This is J71 no. 68269 at West Auckland.   7.7.56

West Auckland was a fairly large depot that was principally concerned with freight work, although in the mid-1950s six A8s were allocated there for local passenger work. It was also home to a number of 0–6–0Ts, among them J71 no. 68254, which was built at Darlington in 1890 and had steam brake only. It was withdrawn in 1960 after completing a remarkable seventy years' service.   7.7.56

The J71 class 0–6–0Ts were built over a period of ten years, all at Darlington Works. No. 68275, photographed at Selby, was completed in January 1892; it remained a steam brake engine throughout its sixty-nine years' service.   23.9.56

When this photograph of J71 no. 68235 was taken at Darlington Works it had already been in service for sixty-nine years. After a further general overhaul, it remained active on shunting duties until November 1960, achieving an amazing seventy-three years' service. No. 68235 was built at Darlington in 1887 and, like many of its classmates, was fitted with steam brake only.   8.7.56

(*Opposite, top*): J72 no. 69020 and 4F 0–6–0 no. 44601 photographed at Darlington. The J72 had been withdrawn from service in December 1963 and had already lost its works plate from the front splasher.   2.5.64

(*Opposite, bottom*): There were few differences among the J72s, but no. 68701 had acquired a shorter and wider-diameter chimney, giving it a very different appearance. This photograph was taken at Normanton, which was a London Midland Region depot. There were three ex-North Eastern 0–6–0Ts in its allocation in the mid-1950s.   13.5.56

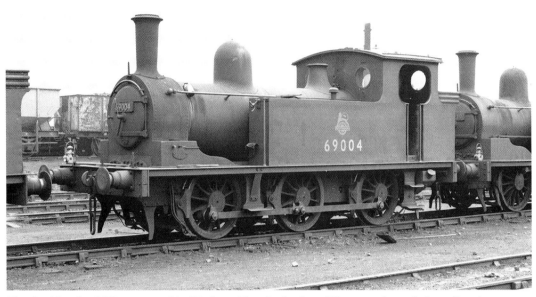

The final batch of J72s appeared in BR days. They had a few differences from their earlier classmates, including twin handles on the smokebox door and modified sanding gear. The sandbox can be seen below the rear of the cab. Group standard buffers were also fitted. No. 69004, a steam brake engine, was photographed at Darlington. Built in 1949, it remained in service until September 1963.　　7.7.56

The J72s were built over a considerable period of time. In total 75 appeared before Grouping in 1923, another 10 in LNER days and the last 28 after nationalisation. This leaves no doubt about their value! No. 68692, seen here at West Auckland, was built in pre-Grouping days. It was completed at Darlington in September 1914 and remained in service until October 1961.　　7.7.56

Small tank locomotives were usually in service for many years. This was certainly not the case with J72 no. 69018 built at Darlington in 1950, well into BR days. It lasted just twelve years, diesel shunters replacing steam. No. 69018 was fitted with a vacuum ejector in January 1957. Photographed at West Aukland. 7.7.56

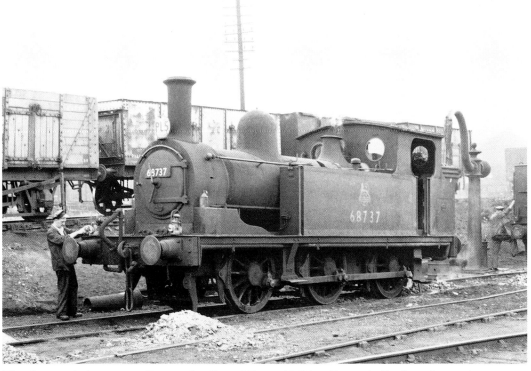

The fireman is busy attending to detail on J72 no. 68737 at Borough Gardens depot. Armstrong, Whitworth & Company built this engine in 1922. It was fitted with a vacuum ejector in June 1955 to enable it to work on empty stock duties. 7.7.56

The J72 class was very similar in appearance to the earlier J71. Introduced in 1898 these engines were remarkable in that twenty-eight were built after nationalisation. No. 68748, seen here at Darlington, was one of ten constructed at Doncaster in 1925. One major difference in the two classes was that the latter had smaller driving wheels. This example was fitted with a vacuum ejector in January 1948; it was withdrawn in January 1959.   8.7.56

(*Opposite*): Dwarfed by the massive coaling plant at Aberdeen Kittybrewster depot, this is J72 no. 68710, one of six to be found there. Although the J72 was a North Eastern Railway design introduced in 1898, the last batch of these very useful locomotives was not completed until 1951, well into British Railways days.   24.8.55

The sub-shed at Hull Alexandra dock came within the jurisdiction of Springhead depot, but despite its lowly status it did have an allocation of its own in the mid-1950s. This included J72 no. 68676, which was built at Darlington in 1898 and completed sixty-two years' service. As can be seen, the engine carried a duty number.   22.5.55

(*Opposite, top*): J72 no. 69001 was the first of the batch built in British Railways days, being completed at Darlington Works in October 1949. It is seen here in immaculate condition, having just returned from a works visit. Increasing numbers of diesel shunters resulted in many steam locomotives becoming redundant, and no. 69001 was condemned in September 1963.   22.5.55

(*Opposite, bottom*): This was the end of the road in more ways than one for J72 no. 68750, photographed at Dumfries. This engine was withdrawn in December 1962 and had already spent several months dumped at the end of this siding when this picture was taken. It was one of a batch built at Doncaster in 1925, and is seen here with an unattractive stovepipe chimney.   6.9.63

One of the East Anglian sugar beet factories that was active in the early 1950s was at Peterborough. (It has since closed.) The depot there had its own locomotives, but pressure of work obliged it to hire J67/2 no. 68496 from Stratford depot. It had been fitted with additional equipment, and carried what appears to be an aerial in front of the chimney. This engine was built in 1890 and withdrawn in May 1956.   4.12.54

J69/1 no. 68576 started life in 1896 as a J67/1. Its Westinghouse pump can be seen, and it was also fitted with a vacuum ejector in 1929. Despite its run-down appearance, with the number and crest barely visible, it remained in service until March 1958.   7.5.55

J69/1 no. 68555 runs through Cambridge station, the rather battered tank sides and unsightly stovepipe chimney doing little to improve its appearance. Built in 1895 as a J67/1, it was rebuilt in 1904, the Westinghouse brake being replaced by steam brake in 1928. It remained in this condition until withdrawal in May 1958.   18.9.54

In the mid-1950s Boston had an allocation of thirty-eight engines, eight of which were 0–6–0Ts of Great Eastern Railway origin. No. 68570 started life in 1896 as a J67/1 and was rebuilt as a J69/1 in 1909. In 1926 the Westinghouse brake was replaced by steam brake and a vacuum ejector was fitted.   13.3.55

Lincoln had a number of 0–6–0Ts in its allocation, among them J69/1 no. 68553. This engine was built in 1895 as a J67/1. During its long service it was rebuilt several times, first as a J69/1, then as a J67/2, and in 1946 it reverted back to a J69/1. During the 1950s diesel shunters took over at a rapidly increasing rate with the result that many small tank engines were made redundant. No. 68553 was withdrawn in December 1958.   14.8.55

One of the tank engines allocated to Cambridge for a considerable period was J69/1 no. 68625. Built at Stratford in 1904, it was equipped with condensing apparatus and Westinghouse brake. In 1932 it was fitted with a vacuum ejector. The condensing gear was removed in LNER days. Withdrawal from service came in January 1959.   9.5.55

J67/2 no. 68597 had been condemned in October 1955, and had already made its last journey from Norwich to Stratford Works. Built in 1900 as a J67/1, it was rebuilt in 1913 as a J69/1 and in 1939 as a J67/2. The principal differences between the J67s and the J69s were in boiler pressure and firebox size.   29.10.55

J69/1 no. 68579 was equipped to work passenger stock and was often to be found at Cambridge on pilot duties. It is seen here in company with LNWR 0–8–0 no. 48898, which had worked in from Bletchley and failed. Also in the picture is a 'Claud' D16/3, one of a number of the class allocated to Cambridge.   28.6.52

J67/1 no. 68509 engaged on shunting work at the engineering yards in Cambridge. In the background is veteran coach no. E 960901. It was by no means uncommon to find old coaches ending their days at engineering yards. No. 68509, built in 1890, had steam brake only. It was withdrawn in March 1954.   28.6.52

(*Opposite, top*): During the 1950s a considerable number of ex-Great Eastern 0–6–0Ts and J15 0–6–0s were running with stovepipe chimneys, many of which were fitted during the Second World War. These did little to improve their appearance, as illustrated by J69/1 no. 68567, seen here standing on what was known locally as 'Cambridge dump'. Built in January 1896 as a J67/1, it was rebuilt to J69/1 in 1913. Withdrawal came in August 1957.   22.8.53

(*Opposite, bottom*): The March station pilot, J68 no. 68664, waits with a parcel van in the station. This engine was built in 1923 with steam brake only, but a vacuum ejector was added in 1935. March depot had more than 150 locomotives in its allocation in 1950, of which just two were small tank engines of the 0–6–0T wheel arrangement. Both were J68s.   8.11.52

During the mid-1950s a considerable number of ex-Great Eastern 0–6–0Ts were to be found at Stratford, among them J67/1 no. 68550, seen here fitted with an unsightly stovepipe chimney. This engine was at one time equipped with condensing equipment but this was removed in 1928. The engine remained in service until July 1961.   7.5.55

(*Opposite*): J69/1 no. 68625 was often employed on station pilot duties at Cambridge. It was fitted with a Westinghouse pump and vacuum ejector. The pumps had a distinctive sound. They also had a tendency to stick, a problem that was often rectified with a sharp blow from a coal hammer or spanner – hence the dents on the casing.   13.7.54

The end of the road for Ipswich J67/1 0–6–0T no. 68606. Withdrawn in March 1953, it is seen here on Stratford's scrap road alongside J70 'Tram' engine no. 68222. Forty-four J67s passed into British Railways ownership, the last being withdrawn in 1957.   7.5.55

J67/1 no. 68493 had been withdrawn several months before this picture was taken at Stratford and it had been dumped at the end of a siding next to the shed used by departmental locomotives. An Ipswich engine in the mid-1950s, it had presumably been towed to Stratford, hence no coupling rods.   7.7.55

Judging by the position of the smokebox door, a fitter had been examining the tubes and tube plate on J68 no. 68663 at Stratford. Originally a steam brake engine, it had a vacuum ejector fitted in February 1937. It remained in service until October 1960.   7.7.55

Locomotives were constantly being shunted around at Stratford, while other engines were moving around under their own steam. This massive shed had over 400 locomotives in its allocation, not including those arriving for works or scrap and those that had already received attention and were waiting to return to their home depots. No. 68588 was originally a J67/1 class, but was converted to a J69/2 in March 1953. It remained in service until May 1958.   7.5.55

J69/1 no. 68630 was built at Stratford in 1904 and was fitted with Westinghouse brake and vacuum ejector. The Westinghouse pump produced its own distinctive sound and had a tendency to stick, often remedied by a hefty wallop from a coal hammer.   7.5.55

The J68 class engines were used for both passenger working and shunting duties. No. 68661, seen here at Stratford, moved to Hitchin in 1956, where it was to remain until December 1959. This steam brake engine had a vacuum ejector added in 1936.   7.5.55

The last Great Eastern 0–6–0Ts were the J68s. Thirty were built in all, ten of which, including no. 68638 seen here at Hitchin, were equipped to work passenger trains. The remaining twenty were all steam brake engines. Note the Westinghouse gear with its battered casing, by no means an unusual sight. No. 68638 spent just two years at Hitchin, before being withdrawn in February 1959.   14.10.56

Most of the 0–6–0Ts allocated to Lincoln depot were J69/1s, including no. 68605, seen here. This class was introduced in 1902 and was a development of the J67 but with higher boiler pressure (180lb as opposed to 160lb) and larger tanks and firebox. Some J69/1s were rebuilt from the earlier design. 25.8.57

Lincoln shed had a number of ex-Great Eastern Railway 0–6–0Ts. Here J69/1 no. 68528 is accompanied by two classmates, nos 68618 and 68599. This former Great Northern Railway depot closed in January 1964; there were only a few locomotives there by this time and most were transferred to Retford. 25.8.57

Ex-Great Eastern Railway 0–6–0Ts were also to be found at several Scottish depots. This is J69/1 no. 68551, fitted with a stovepipe chimney, at Dundee. This locomotive was built at Stratford in 1895 as a J67/1 and rebuilt to J69/1 in January 1904. Withdrawal came in May 1958.   23.8.55

The Darlington Works pilot, J94 no. 68060, was one of the batch built by Hudswell, Clarke & Company in 1945/6. Steam locomotives were still going through the works in 1964, although time was rapidly running out for them in favour of diesel power.   2.5.64

J94 no. 68037 was allocated to Darlington for a number of years. This Vulcan Foundry-built engine carried the WD number 75322. In January 1949 it was fitted with an extended bunker. The J94s were powerful locomotives that proved to be a very useful purchase by the LNER.   7.7.56

Several of the J94 class 0–6–0STs were sold after withdrawal. No. 68020, built by W.G. Bagnall & Company and seen here at Doncaster, went to the National Coal Board three months after it was withdrawn and ended its days at Askean Colliery in 1970.   24.6.56

The design chosen to fulfill the Ministry of Supply's urgent need for shunting locomotives to operate on the continent during the Second World War was the Hunslet 18in inside cylinder 0–6–0ST, albeit with some modifications. Locomotives of this type were built by a number of private companies. The Hunslet Engine Company constructed no. 68008, seen here at Darlington Works.   7.7.56

Sixteen of the J94 class that went into LNER stock were built by Hudswell Clarke & Company, one of them being no. 68062, seen here at Newport with two of its classmates. Built in 1945, this engine completed almost twenty years' service. Note the extra set of steps midway and the additional handrail.   8.7.56

One of the companies involved with the construction of the WD Austerity 0–6–0STs for the Ministry of Supply was W.G. Bagnall & Company of Stafford. Sixteen of these engines were to become LNER class J94s. No. 68058, seen here at Sunderland, was completed in February 1946 as WD no. 75270. It was never fitted with an extended bunker and was withdrawn in October 1962.   8.7.56

In 1946/7 the LNER purchased seventy-five ex-Ministry of Supply 0–6–0STs, built by seven different private companies, and these became class J94. No. 68043, seen here at Darlington, was completed by the Vulcan Foundry in July 1945. This engine has an additional footstep and handrail on the saddle tank. It was among the last members of the class in service and was withdrawn in May 1965.   8.7.56

In the early 1950s there were no J94s to be found at the London end of the East Coast main line, but in the closing years of the decade five were allocated to Hornsey. Here they worked alongside the large stud of J50 0–6–0Ts that had replaced the ex-GNR J52 class 0–6–0STs. No. 68022 is seen here at Doncaster, where it was to remain until withdrawal in September 1960.   25.8.57

The extended bunker fitted to J94 no. 68074 in July 1950 can be clearly seen in this picture, which was taken while the locomotive was stored at Immingham. No. 68074 was one of the batch built by Andrew Barclay & Company in 1945/6, and was allocated the WD number 71535. It was returned to traffic, remaining at Immingham until transferring to Colwick in 1960, from where it was withdrawn in October 1962.   25.8.57

In July 1952 the steam working on the Wisbech & Upwell Tramway was taken over completely by Drewry diesel mechanical 0–6–0s. As a safeguard one J70 0–6–0T, no. 68222, was retained as a spare until March 1953. During this time it was used on several occasions. The remainder of the engines moved to March. Among them was no. 68223, seen here in company with Y6 0–4–0T no. 68083. The engine was complete so presumably had travelled to March under its own steam. It was not withdrawn until July 1955, seeing further service on Yarmouth Docks.

8.11.52

Several of the J70 'Tram' engines stored at March were to see further service shunting on docks. Sadly this was not the case for no. 68217, which was withdrawn in March 1953. Y6 no. 68083, the next in line, was not lucky either, being condemned in November 1952.   8.11.52

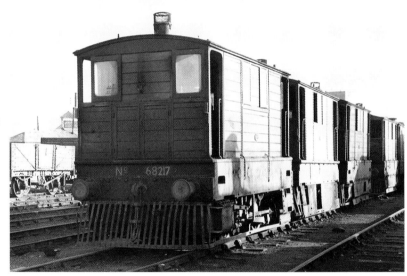

It is a great pity that none of these ex-Great Eastern Railway J70 'Tram' engines made it into preservation. This is no. 68225 on the scrap road at Stratford. It had ended its days at Ipswich working on the docks. Built in 1921, it remained in service until March 1955.   7.5.55

J70 'Tram' engine no. 68222 was the last to work on the Wisbech & Upwell Tramway, having been retained for a year after the diesels took over. It was then sent to Ipswich. Withdrawal was in January 1955, and I photographed it several months later at Stratford Works. Twelve of these engines were built, between 1903 and 1921, and the class became extinct in 1955.   7.5.55

The J70 'Tram' engines could be driven from either end. They were designed for use on public roads and the regulations required them to be fitted with cowcatchers, warning bells and protective covers over the wheels. In addition, spark arresters were fitted and governors limited their speed to 8mph. Towards the end of their service some of these items were removed, except when they were used on roads. A Colchester engine, no. 68226 is seen here at Stratford Works, awaiting the scrapman's torch.   29.10.55

The J70 class 'Tram' engines will be best remembered for their service on the Wisbech & Upwell Tramway, where five were still working in 1952 when they were replaced by diesels. No. 68223 was allocated to Yarmouth Vauxhall and used on dock shunting. It was withdrawn in July 1955. It is seen here at Stratford Works, still lettered British Railways, and awaiting scrapping.   29.02.55

J66 0–6–0T no. 8387 never received its BR number, being withdrawn in February 1951. It is seen here at New England a month before withdrawal, still lettered LNER and fitted with an unattractive short stovepipe chimney. Built at Stratford in 1888, this engine had a long working life. It was the only J66 allocated to New England at this time.   28.1.51

For many years J66 0–6–0T no. 68383 was allocated to Cambridge, but it moved to Staveley for its final period in service. When this picture was taken it had been withdrawn and was awaiting scrapping. This engine completed sixty-seven years' service and was the last of the class, although three J66s still survived in service stock.   29.10.55

The sidings to the north of the shed building at Cambridge, often referred to locally as 'the dump', was always a magnet for enthusiasts. Here you could find engines awaiting repair and visitors passing through to and from works, as well as engines waiting for their next duty, as was the case with J66 no. 68383.   28.6.52

J66 no. 68383 was allocated to Cambridge depot for a number of years. This class numbered fifty locomotives, including one in service stock, and all were built at Stratford between 1886 and 1888. Many were withdrawn before nationalisation, and only nineteen were handed over. No. 68383 was the last in service, with the exception of three in departmental stock at Stratford Works.   28.6.52

The huge complex at Stratford included a small shed for departmental locomotives. On the right is departmental no. 36, a J66 class 0–6–0T. Formerly no. 68378, built in 1888, this engine was withdrawn in September 1952 and moved into service stock two months later. It continued in this role until January 1959. Barely visible on the left is departmental no. 31, another J66.   7.5.55.

One engine that became well known to me in the early 1950s was J66 no. 68383, seen here awaiting scrapping at Stratford in company with Y4 0–4–0T no. 68125. This J66 was allocated to Cambridge for many years but its last period in service was at Staveley, from where it was withdrawn in October 1955. The last member of the class in running stock, this veteran completed sixty-seven years' service.   13.11.55

Ten J73 class 0–6–0Ts were built at Gateshead Works in 1891/2. These small but powerful locomotives were principally intended to work on the difficult lines on both sides of the Tyne, replacing less powerful 0–6–0Ts. In 1940 these three J73s – nos 68357, 68356 and 68362 – were transferred to Selby, where they were to end their working lives. All were withdrawn in 1957/8.   23.9.56

The short-wheelbase J88s were introduced in 1904 for dock shunting and for use on lines with tight curves. Thirty-five were constructed at Cowlairs in batches, the last in 1919. Their tall chimneys and outside cylinders made these engines distinctive. No. 68335, built in 1909, was one of two to receive vacuum ejectors, all the others being steam brake only. This picture was taken as the engine was trundling back to its home shed, Thornton.   24.8.55

(*Opposite*): J73 no. 68359 was built in 1892 at Gateshead Works and was withdrawn in December 1959. It is seen here at West Hartlepool shed, and the picture clearly illustrates the limited clearance typical of many depot entrances. There are warning signs on both sides but they are barely visible through the soot and grime. Some of the brickwork certainly required attention. Just outside the door was an ash-pit.   8.7.56

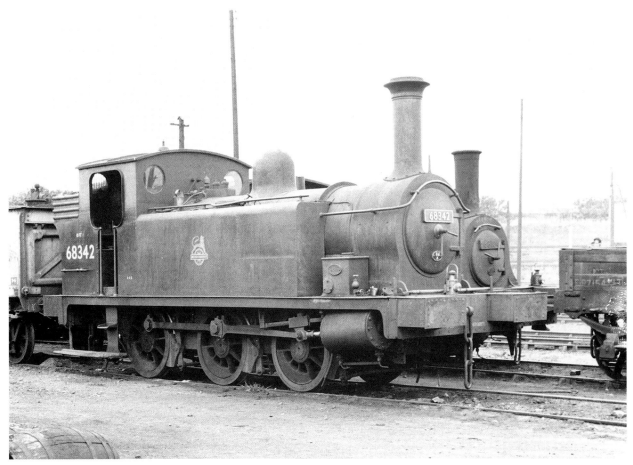

The small (3ft 9in diameter) wheels and short wheelbase of the J88 class can be clearly seen in this picture, as can the very distinctive tall chimney. Designed for shunting in difficult locations, they were classified 0F. No. 68342 is seen here at South Leith, a sub-shed of St Margaret's, where two J88s could normally be found.   21.8.55

(*Opposite, top*): The J88s were fitted with solid buffers to prevent 'locking' when shunting around tight curves. No. 68320 is receiving attention at the 'old tank' roundhouse at St Margaret's. Eight of the class were allocated to the depot, although several were outstationed at sub-sheds. No. 68320 was the first of the class to be built, being completed in December 1904.   21.8.55

(*Opposite, bottom*): Two North British veterans at South Leith. J88 no. 68342 stands in company with a Y9 0–4–0ST. The wooden tender of another Y9 can be seen on the right. Both these classes were fitted with solid buffers.   21.8.55

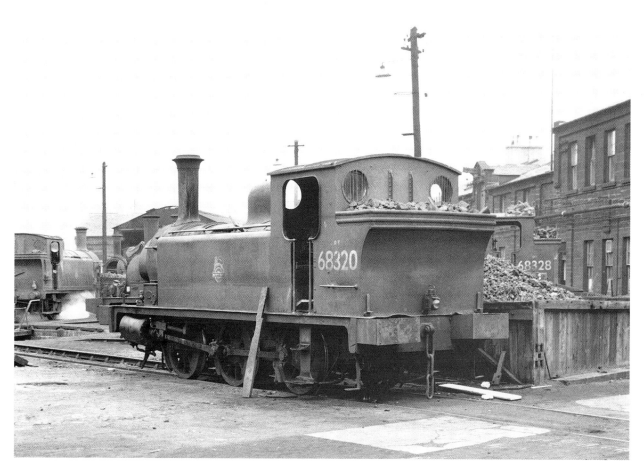

Standing on a short siding in the bleak surroundings of Seafield on a cold Monday morning, J88 class no. 68325 was waiting to be prepared for its next duty. In the background is the coaling plant, with a loaded wagon ready for use.   21.8.55

At some stage J88 no. 68345, seen here at Dunfermline, had been fitted with a spark arrester, the rim of which still remained on the chimney. Dunfermline depot had three J88s in its allocation.   22.8.55

Three J88s were allocated to Polmont depot, where no. 68354 is seen engaged in shunting work. Introduced in 1904, these engines were the standard North British Railway dock shunters. Thirty-five were built, all of which passed into British Railways ownership. No. 68354 remained in service until September 1960.   22.8.55

J88 no. 68321 in the spacious yards of Thornton shed, which had a long association with these engines. These locomotives were instantly recognisable with their tall chimneys, small wheels and outside cylinders. No. 68321 was the second of the class to be built, being completed at Cowlairs in December 1904; withdrawal came in December 1958.   24.8.55

Twenty class A7 4–6–2Ts were built at Darlington in 1910/11. Although principally designed for trip workings, these locomotives spent much of their time shunting in marshalling yards around the north-east. During the 1950s most of the class were to be found in the Hull area, working to and from the docks. No. 69784 is seen here at Springhead shed. It remained in service until March 1956.   22.5.55

Hull Dairycoates was the largest shed in the North Eastern Region, with 130 locomotives in its allocation in the mid-1950s. It consisted of a huge roundhouse with six turntables. No. 69107 is seen here in a quiet spot awaiting its next duty. This locomotive was withdrawn in December 1957.   22.5.55

N10 0–6–2T no. 69106 awaits its next turn of duty in the depths of Tyne Dock shed in company with J72 0–6–0T no. 68706. Twenty N10s were built but only three were still in service at the start of the 1960s. No. 69106 was not among them, having been withdrawn in March 1958.   7.7.56

N10 no. 69104 at Hull Dairycoates. This engine was built at Darlington in 1902. It was withdrawn in March 1958, ending its days where it had started, Darlington, the following month.   22.5.55

In the mid-1950s five of these ex-North Eastern Railway N10 0–6–2Ts were to be found at Hull Dairycoates depot. No. 69104 is seen here carrying the duty 22 plate. This twenty-strong class was introduced in 1902; all were taken into British Railways stock.   22.5.55

J77 no. 68391, pictured inside West Auckland shed, started life as an 0–4–4 passenger tank engine. Built by Neilson & Company in 1874, it was rebuilt as an 0–6–0T at Darlington in 1908. It was nearing the end of its days when this picture was taken and was withdrawn the following year. The Neilson-built engines had circular cab windows.   7.7.56

A number of the J77 class 0–6–0Ts were fitted with vacuum ejectors and carriage-heating equipment. This was the case with no. 68423, seen here at Darlington. This engine was built at Gateshead in 1878 as an 0–4–4T; withdrawal came in November 1957.   7.7.56

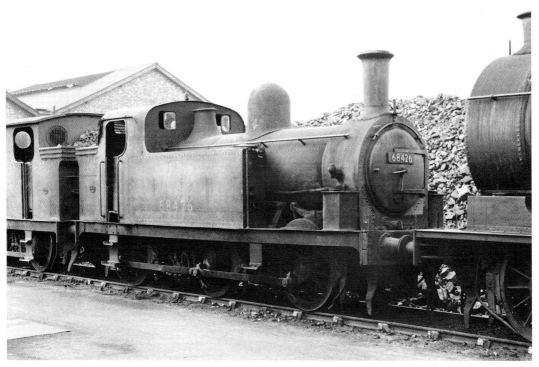

The LNER class J77 0–6–0Ts were all rebuilds, and forty-six of the sixty rebuilt in this way were still in service at nationalisation. This engine, no. 68426, was completed at Darlington in 1879 and rebuilt as an 0–6–0T at York in March 1901. It remained in service until August 1957. It was photographed at North Blyth.   7.7.56

J77 no. 68399, seen here at Blyth, was constructed by Hawthorn & Company as an 0–4–4T in 1875 and rebuilt as an 0–6–0T at York in March 1902. Rebuilding to class J77 was carried out at York and Darlington. No. 68399 remained in service until April 1958.   7.7.56

Six examples of the J83 class were allocated to Thornton depot. These were powerful but easily maintained locomotives. Only one of the forty built did not make it into British Railways ownership. No. 68451, constructed in 1900, completed fifty-eight years' service. Note the coal lying on the cab roof.   24.8.55

The ex-North British Railway J83 class was designed for heavy shunting transfer and trip working. Forty were constructed in 1900/1, twenty each by Neilson, Reid & Company and Sharp, Stewart & Company. All were rebuilt shortly after Grouping. The majority of the class had steam brake only. No. 68453 is seen here at Thornton. It was built in 1901 by Neilson, Reid & Company, and remained in service until October 1962. 24.8.55

Looking at this picture it is certainly not readily apparent that these two locomotives were built forty-nine years apart! J83 no. 68448 on the left was built by Neilson, Reid & Company in 1900, while the J72 was one of the batch completed at Darlington in 1949 (albeit to a design first introduced in 1898!). This picture was taken at South Leith. 21.8.55

Forty J83 0–6–0Ts were built. Some of them were equipped to work passenger stock, including
no. 68473, seen here at Haymarket shed. Engines with these fittings were generally employed as
carriage pilots. No. 68473 had recently received works attention, but it was to remain in service for
less than a year after this picture was taken.   21.5.55

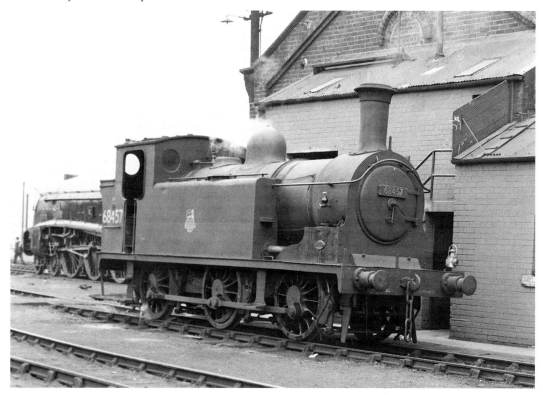

Five J83s were allocated to Haymarket depot, including no. 68457. In the background the well-known
A4 no. 60009 *Union of South Africa* is being prepared for its next duty.   22.8.55

The best day to visit the sub-shed at South Leith was a Sunday, as all the locomotives would be present. They were supplied by St Margaret's depot and changed on a regular basis. Here J83 no. 68454 and a Y9 0–4–0ST were ready to be steamed for the start of another busy week.   21.8.55

For an engine to spend its entire working life on the same duty was very unusual. J83 no. 68464, seen here at St Margaret's, was one that did so, working the 'Leith Walk No. 3 pilot' duty. Sharp, Stewart & Company built this engine in 1901, and it remained in service until March 1958.   21.8.55

J83 no. 68465, seen here at Dundee, spent fifty-six years on mundane but very important shunting work. The J83s were introduced in 1900, with the first batch built by Neilson, Reid & Company, changing to Sharp, Stewart & Company in 1901. 23.8.55

(*Opposite*): Eastfield Glasgow was one of the largest sheds in the Scottish Region, and it would have been odd if it had not had some J83s in its allocation. No. 68468, built by Sharp, Stewart & Company in 1901, was one of six to be found there. The J83s were mostly steam brake engines and were used for shunting work throughout Scotland, in the area that was formerly North British and later LNER territory. 26.8.55

Eastfield was among the best of the Scottish Region depots for enthusiasts owing to the wide range of locomotive types to be found there. Here J83 no. 68447 stands in company with another member of the class. In the background can be seen B1 no. 61101, and part of the smokebox door of K2 no. 61789 *Loch Laidon*.   26.8.55

(*Opposite*): Colwick depot had a number of J52 0–6–0STs in its allocation in the mid-1950s, among them no. 68777. This engine was classified as J53 class by the LNER but was rebuilt as a J52 in December 1931. It is fitted with condensing gear. Note the dent and what appears to be a hole in the second dome. Time had nearly run out for this engine when this picture was taken as it was withdrawn in November 1954.   4.4.54

Colwick depot had a sizeable allocation of J52s during the early 1950s, among them no. 68814. This engine was completed at Doncaster in October 1897 and remained in service until November 1955. Locomotives were certainly built to last in those days, especially shunting locomotives, which regularly clocked up fifty-five years or more.   4.4.55

(*Opposite, top*): In the mid-1950s twenty of the veteran ex-Great Northern Railway J52 0–6–0STs were to be found at Kings Cross shed. Shortly after nationalisation the figure rose to thirty, but by 1959 just one remained and the class became extinct in 1961. Fortunately one has survived into preservation. One thing I shall always remember about these engines was their sharp exhaust note. No. 68827 was withdrawn in January 1956.   3.1.54

(*Opposite, bottom*): In the early 1950s a considerable number of J52s were still to be seen in the London area, while others were to be found at several Eastern Region sheds. No. 68843 was a Doncaster engine. Massive inroads were made into the class during the mid-1950s, but no. 68843 survived until April 1957.   23.9.56

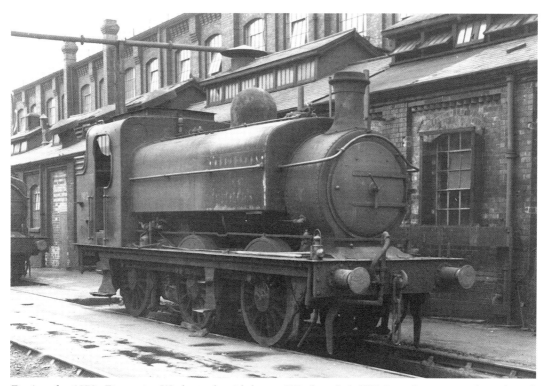

During the 1950s Doncaster Works took withdrawn J52 class 0–6–0STs into departmental stock and used them for shunting in the works area. No. 68858 was withdrawn from running stock in December 1955 and became departmental no. 2 in March 1956. It is seen here in far from ideal light conditions in the works yard.   10.11.57

J52 no. 68760 was built as a J53 at Doncaster in 1893 and rebuilt to a J52 in 1923. A number of the class were fitted with condensing gear, which was required when working over the Metropolitan widened lines; in a number of cases it was later blanked off. During the early and mid-1950s huge inroads were made in the class.   7.11.54

Two condensing J52s at Doncaster shed, before being transferred to the works scrap road. Nos 68791 and 68760 were built by Neilson & Company and Doncaster Works in 1896 and 1893 respectively. Both were withdrawn in November 1954.   7.11.54

The ashpits at Doncaster shed were always busy as a steady stream of locomotives arrived for servicing. J52 no. 68886 was one of the last of the class to be built, being completed at Doncaster in February 1909. It remained in service until November 1957.   7.11.54

Doncaster shed still had a number of J52s in its allocation in the 1950s, including no. 68778, which was fitted with condensing gear. Built at Doncaster as a J53, it was rebuilt as a J52 in 1924 and withdrawn in July 1957.   7.11.54

(*Opposite, top*): New England depot had an overhead water system that enabled locomotives to refill on several of the shed roads. Part of this system can be seen in this picture of J52 no. 68817. The engine was built by R. Stephenson & Company in 1899 and was withdrawn in 1958.   13.3.55

(*Opposite, bottom*): On Sunday mornings in the mid-1950s locomotives en route to Doncaster Works or other depots were often to be seen at Huntingdon, mostly taking water there, as was the case with J52 no. 68819. This engine was transferring to another shed, as it was not withdrawn until June 1956.   6.2.55

Locomotives built in Victorian times were certainly built to last. J52 no. 68885, was completed at Doncaster in February 1909. While some of its classmates achieved over sixty years' service, no. 68885 managed only forty-seven, largely because of the influx of new diesel shunters.   25.8.57

(*Opposite, top*): Locomotives under repair were often to be seen in the yard at Doncaster and this is J52 no. 68882 in a very run-down condition and with its coupling rods removed. Constructed at Doncaster in 1908, it was to complete fifty years' service before withdrawal. Three private companies also built members of this class.   23.9.56

(*Opposite, bottom*): The Great Northern Railway works plates fitted to shunting locomotives varied from brass to cast versions. This one was carried by J52 no. 68810, built at Doncaster and completed in October 1897. It was allocated to Colwick when this picture was taken, remaining in service until November 1955.   4.4.54

The first member of the J52 class was withdrawn in 1936, but 133 passed into British Railways ownership. In the early 1950s a steady stream made their way to Doncaster for scrapping. No. 68888, the penultimate member of the class, was built in 1909 and withdrawn in 1957. It is seen here on the scrap road at Doncaster Works.   10.11.57

(*Opposite, top*): Still with its front number plate and shed plate fitted, J52 no. 68832, formerly of Kings Cross, was photographed at Doncaster Works awaiting scrapping. Most of the London engines made their final journey under their own steam.   10.11.57

(*Opposite, bottom*): Work had already started on J52 no. 68874, seen here standing on the Doncaster scrap road. The smokebox door, dome cover and front steps had already been removed. Built in 1905, this engine was withdrawn in October 1957 and cut up the following month.   10.11.57

New England J52 no. 68844 awaits cutting up at Doncaster Works scrap road. It still carried its front number plate and shedcode, but one of the cab spectacle glasses had been removed. This engine had been condemned just a month before this picture was taken.   7.11.54

For many years the J52s allocated to New England depot were a familiar sight around Peterborough. These two, nos 68850 and 68844, were both from this depot and presumably had worked up under their own steam together.   7.11.54